Control Your Inner Trader

by LR Thomas

Trading the financial markets has large potential rewards but also large potential risks. You must be aware of the risks and be willing to accept them in order to invest in the financial markets. Don't trade with money you can't afford to lose. No representation is made that any account is likely to or will achieve profits or losses similar to any information found in this book. The past performance of any trading system or methodology does not necessarily indicate future results.

Table of Contents

The Challenge of Trading

Most books about trading psychology are very complex: this book is not one of them. Most books about trading psychology describe the difficulties faced by traders but fall short of describing processes to deal with those problems; again, this book is not one of those type of books.

This book outlines the challenges traders face with their psychology and then outlines simple strategies to deal with each of those challenges.

The reason I can cover these in a book when I don't know you personally is that the challenges of trading tend to evoke the same behaviors.
Let me list those behaviors now so you can see what I mean.

Problem Behaviours in Trading

Entering a trade when there is no trade to take.
Frequently missing trades that you should have taken.
Entering trades too late.
Entering trades too early.
Revenge trading, where you lose control and start trying to make back losses.
Risking too much on a trade.
Risking too little on a trade.
Trading outside strategy.
Trading without a stop loss.
Moving a stop loss further away
Trading with too tight a stop loss.
Taking profits too early.
Taking profits too late.
Trading too many strategies and mixing them up.
Trading too many time frames and mixing them up
Trading too many pairs.
Being too influenced by other traders
Buying trading course after trading course
Searching for the Holy Grail trading system
Frozen Trigger finger (fear of entering trades)

All the above issues are symptoms of a wrong trading mind set, so why does that happen and what can we do about it.
Let me start with the foundational attitude needed to become a 'Pro' trader. Notice I said 'Pro' trader, I didn't say winning trader. There is a profound difference in attitude between a trader working at increasing professionalism and a trader who wants to be a 'winning' trader. So why should you work at being a pro trader?

Turning Pro

In his book 'The War of Art' a book which I highly recommend you buy, Stephen Pressfield describes the difference between an amateur and a professional. Firstly, a professional is not defined by the result of their behaviour but by their seriousness about the process. They have to overcome their inner resistance which is their worst enemy.

'Turning Pro' as defined in his excellent book is a decision to commit no matter what the result. To accept that things will be hard and miserable and boring, but your job is to turn up and do your 'work' to the best of your ability.

Pressfield defines 'work' as any activity that improves your life over the long term but in the short term is uncomfortable. However, I think his analogy is more applicable to a creative act which is his writing but could easily describe the act of trading. Throughout this book I will describe the desired trading mentality as 'turning pro'.

Trading is the ultimate creative act, our trading systems whether they are our own design or not, require us to make a judgement that we know is ultimately subjective. We decide to risk money on our ideas, and we have to decide on when to get in and out of the markets. This requires an independent mind set and a commitment to excellence that most people never make. In other words, you have to treat your creative act like a profession. But unlike most professions, you make the rules. You turn pro when you abide by the rules you have made, even when you don't yet know if they are valid.

The problem is that many people get into trading as a way of obtaining freedom from a job or profession. They don't want more professionalism, they want less. They don't want to make rules and stick to them, they want creative freedom. They don't want boring and miserable; they want exciting and happy. These attitudes form their foundational mind set when they get into trading. Is it any wonder that they trade impulsively when their foundation is all messed up?

They look to trading to provide what they are not getting from their lives; they ask of trading what trading is not able to give. They want trading to fill the hole in their lives and to be profitable. Trading cannot do that. Trading is just trading!

If you look to trading to get excitement then trading can give you excitement, but don't expect to be profitable if what you are really looking for is excitement.

If you are looking to trading to fill your time then trading can take up every hour of your time, but don't expect to be profitable if what you are really looking for is a way to fill your time.

If you are looking for a new challenge in life then trading can challenge you as you have never been challenged before, but it does not mean you will be profitable.

Do you see where I am going with this, if you got into trading for the wrong reasons, then now is the time to admit it to yourself and consider whether you really want to get further involved in trading. Why should you consider this? Because a professional trader is not looking for excitement or challenge or a way to spend their time, they are simply looking for opportunities to profit in the market.

That is their job, and they have to have the exquisite patience to wait for the right opportunity, to wait for the right entry, to wait for the trade to play out, to wait to get to break even and to wait to take profits.

Waiting... waiting is not exciting, it is the most boring thing you can do, and it also encourages anxiety among traders who are not pro. This anxiety is what causes behaviours

such as taking trades that aren't there or entering a trade too early. Are you prepared to wait, because in trading that is how you will spend the vast majority of your time?
Compare trading to travelling on a bus, firstly when you wait for a bus you know you will have to wait, you accept it. If another bus comes along without your number on the front you let it go by, you don't think 'I don't know if another bus will come along so I better take this bus'. When you do get on the right bus, how do you then spend your time? You don't keep looking out the window to check if the bus is moving, you while away your time reading or doing work or chatting while you wait for the bus to finish its journey. You fully accept the bus journey may be long, you may try and alleviate the boredom by doing some other things while the bus is doing its' thing, but you don't try to micromanage the bus journey.
If this analogy doesn't 'speak' to you, then what about fishing. When you see fishermen waiting for the right bite to come and sitting on the bank does that look exciting, yet that is the type of activity that trading really involves.
(Here I will digress for a little and say that this was my biggest problem, I just couldn't wait! I have attention deficit disorder and I have always had problems of impulse control, but I would not accept it. I just tried harder but if anything, that made the problem worse.
The problem was easily solved by only trading the larger time frames. No more long hours spent staring at the screen! I am not by nature a fisherman.)

Another reason that a lot of people get into trading is that they think it is a route to fast riches, or 'get rich quick'. They may have little money from their job, or they need to replace their income and because they have this belief about trading, they do things in their trading that a professional trader wouldn't do.

They bet too much on their trades, they are careless about their entries; they let their profits run too far and get whipsawed by the price, losing the profits they have made. They get caught up in revenge trading and eventually get margined out.
Can you see how the wrong beliefs about trading can cause certain types of behaviours? The truth about trading is that most of the rich traders you hear about get rich by trading money for other people.
The richest traders are hedge fund managers and people who own trading houses, highly paid bank traders and other high paid traders at the top of their profession. They earn the big money by getting a performance percentage.
If you want to make big money from the markets, the best route is to become a profitable and professional trader with a proven track record and then go work for a fund or set up your own fund.
Can you see the different behaviours it would evoke if your goal were to become a profitable trader and build a track record so you could attract investment, rather than use trading itself as a vehicle for making fast money?
Retail traders working from home, overall can make a very good living from the markets if they are successful, however few of them are mega rich.
When you read about these work-at-home traders you will also see they usually took quite a few years to build up to that level.
The advantage that a retail trader has over the hedge fund manager or bank trader is that they have no accountability to investors or bosses.
This brings me to my next point. Another reason people want to become traders is to have freedom and independence. They are sick of having a boss, or they may have been fired from their job and they want to call the shots in their own life.
Now up to a point trading can provide freedom and independence. You are location independent, anywhere you can get an internet connection is suitable for trading. You have

no boss, no employees, no stock, no suppliers, and no office politics, none of the usual hassles of working for a boss or running your own business.

The trouble comes when the beliefs about the type of freedom provided by the markets spill over into a trading system. This leads to behaviours like ignoring the rules of your system, missing trades because you fail to check the charts at the appropriate times, chopping and changing between systems, adding one part of a system to another system. After all, if the market gives you complete freedom to do what you want then what difference does it make, right?

The truth is that trading can become a harsh task master depending on what trading system you choose, the way to get more freedom is to choose a system with a great amount of freedom built in, such as an end of day or four-hour system. (My trading systems Trade around Your Job and The 10XROI Trading System are designed for this).

Many traders make the mistake of choosing a system that requires the same time attendance as a full-time job, or worse. If you are based in the US and you want to trade the London Open, then you have to get up in the early hours of the morning. This is fine if you accept this, but if there is an internal conflict because you are looking for greater freedom in your life then you will indulge in self sabotaging behaviours that can ruin your trading.

The other reason these types of intense day trading systems are difficult to adhere to is due to the amount of time you can maintain emotional self-control. (I go into this in more depth later in the book).

Therefore, the areas of trading where you have freedom are in the type of trading system you choose, the instruments you trade and the location you choose.

The areas of trading where you have no freedom are to do with sticking to the rules of the trading system you have chosen, sticking to the money management plan you have chosen, keeping detailed records in order to practice Kaizen (continuous compounding improvement)

So, the first stage to turning pro is to fully accept the true nature of trading, what it is and what it isn't...

If you can accept this, you have reached the first stage of becoming a professional trader.

The second stage is to decide whether you truly want to commit to becoming a professional trader. (Remember that doesn't mean a winning trader that means professional in your attitude)

Why is it important to differentiate between being a winning trader and being a professional trader?

The reason is that one is completely within our control, and one is completely outside our control. The true professional has faith that if she does her part then the numbers will play out and she will by default become profitable, but she has no control over whether the next trade will be a winner or a loser. Therefore, to have as a goal to be winning trader or even a profitable trader is inappropriate, that should be built into the trading system you are using.

The goal is to be a professional trader and execute your system as it was meant to be executed when you designed it. That is the only thing you can control and is the only thing that will ensure that your trading becomes profitable over the long term.

Therefore, most of your time and focus should be spent on the execution of your system, combined with recording the results. The mind-set is one of Kaizen which is Japanese for "improvement" or "change for the best" and refers to philosophy or practices that focus upon continuous improvement of processes.

Each change in itself may be small, but the compounded effect of many small improvements leads to huge improvements overall. For example, let's say you have a win loss ratio of 40%, that is you win four out of ten trades. You discover through keeping rigorous records that you have more winners when you short than when you take longs. You decide to only take shorts and increase your win loss ratio to 55%.

You also find that your normal take profit is 1-2, you intend to stay in the trade longer to take bigger profits, but you always get impatient and scared of losing your winnings and exit early in the trade.

Through back testing you find that most of your winning trades would have easily given you a 1-4 reward if you had only stayed in the trade. You put in place techniques (which I will give you later) to stop yourself trying to micro-manage the trade and put in fixed exits of 1-4 Risk Reward Ratio.

What has now happened to your profits, well you turned an unprofitable trading system which only had a 40%-win rate and a 1-2 Risk reward to a very profitable system with a 55%-win rate and a 1-4 Risk Reward, just by making 2 changes! This is the work of the professional trader, constant improvement of their performance.

Before you go any further in this book, I advise you to take some time to really digest what I have said. Do you really want to commit yourself to turning pro?

It may not be what you really want and there is no shame in that. I listened to an interview once by a trader who had over a 10-year period lost over a million pounds in trading. He'd had a successful business but got the trading bug and because he had the money, he just kept blowing out his accounts.

He was still trading 10 years later but I wonder if looking back he would really have chosen that journey. It seems obvious to me that he wanted challenge in his life, and he used trading as a vehicle to get it.

This is what you do not want to happen in your trading career!

Talent Versus Hard Work

So have you decided you want to be a professional trader? Yes?
Then let me ask you another harder question, are you naturally talented at trading?
The prevailing overview is that trading is a learned skill, and you don't need talent. That anyone can learn to become anything if they try hard enough. I disagree with this view. I am naturally talented in English, I always got A in my exams without any study, I was also very talented in telephone sales in my younger days, I am not naturally talented in trading.
Some people are naturally talented creatives, some are great singers. When you see real talent you recognise it easily, even in its raw state. That is the job of a talent scout.
If that is the case, then why shouldn't this apply to trading as well? Talent makes acquiring a skill a whole lot easier. How can you recognise talent in trading?
By the amount of time it takes to acquire the skills and mind-set needed to perform!
Talented traders need a lot less time. If you hear about a trader who became profitable in less than 2 years, then you can be sure that trader has talent.
Now you can become a profitable trader without talent, but it will be a longer harder journey. The woman in this video took 10 years to get to the stage of having a fund of over $140,000,00
https://traderselfcontrol.com/resources/

The 10,000 Hour Rule

This brings me on to my next point, the 10,000-hour rule. In his excellent book 'Outliers' Malcolm Gladwell talks about the 10,000-hour rule. He cites a study that looked at what top professional musicians did differently from musicians who just went on to become music teachers.
This study found that talent was not a factor, what made the difference was the amount and type of practice. The pro-musicians practiced much, much more than the less successful musicians.
Additionally, they practiced those areas which would stretch them and make them grow as musicians, the difficult, boring stuff, whereas the less committed musicians practiced what felt more comfortable.
So, what is the conclusion to this, my view is that some traders have a natural talent that helps shorten the time taken to becoming profitable, however evidence shows that most people who reach the top of their profession do so through having the equivalent of 10,000 hours of the right sort of challenging and stretching practice.
Either way this shows that if you are dedicated you can become successful at trading.
Are you committed? Ok, then let's begin.

Creating Your Psychological Foundation

For many traders who have been trading in an out-of-control fashion for a period of time, they may need to start over and so I am going to start this with that in mind. If you have been trading like this my first advice to you is STOP TRADING NOW!

You need to clear your head and start with a clean slate. By stopping trading for a few weeks and then committing to this process, you can reboot your brain and start over.

Your Trading System

If you have problems because you have too many systems on the go; if you keep skipping from system to system and buying new courses, it's time to stop.
The reason traders do this is because of a fear of missing out on the latest greatest system being peddled.
They underestimate the intense focus it takes just to make one strategy profitable. They also equate more systems with more opportunities and more opportunities with making more money.
The problem is that your human brain is limited in the number of things it can focus on at one time. When you try to trade too many time frames, currency pairs or systems you lose clarity, and when you lose clarity, you can't trade successfully.

The other issue is that traders try to trade systems and time frames that don't suit their personality and lifestyle. They think because another trader is profitable trading that system then they will be too. However, nothing could be further from the truth, you must trade a system that suits you and discard anything that doesn't.
I made this mistake a while back; I bought a course created by a fantastic short-term trader with a 94% documented win rate. However, I can't trade like her, I have not the patience to stare at the screen during the day. Her method was so different from my own swing trading method that I didn't even bother to follow through with testing the system. I just resolved to stick to what I was good at and not make that mistake again.

How do you know which type of system is right for you? It is the system you seem to have the most success with, that is the easiest and feels most natural.

For me it is the daily and four-hour charts and using the hourly charts to fine tune entries. (If you are interested in my methods, try my book the 10XROI trading System or my other books Trade around Your Job and my trade management system that can turn a 1-10 ROI Trade up to a 1-30 ROI trade, Pyramid Your Trades to Profit. They can be found on my author page or see the resource section at the end of this book).

When you have one system that works for you, focus on that system and nothing else until you are consistently trading that system to as near perfection as you can.
What is vital is to measure everything, so you see where your most profitable trades are and where you lose money. For example, you may find that you win many more shorts than longs, so then stop trading longs with the system. Immediately you have improved your profitability.
What type of things can you test? trading shorts only, trading longs only, entry type, entry time of day, days of the week, size of stop and size of take profit, type of entry, and type of exit and much more.
You need to be constantly testing to find the most profitable way to execute your method. So, you see why it is more important to find a method that suits you than a fantastically profitable method. You can always tweak to produce a higher return, but you can't turn a natural swing trader into a great scalper!

There is no real need to add more systems unless you have very few opportunities in your current one, as if you have a winning system, you can make enough money to cover all your wants and needs.

If you do add another system, then look for something that easily slots into your current system, so your brain has as little adaptation as possible. What do I mean by that? Well in my 10XROI System I use the daily charts to find specific entry setups and use the one-hour charts to confirm and enter the trade.

In my Trade around Your Job system, I am still using daily charts and I am using the same set of circumstances on the daily chart, but the entries are different, and I use the close of the four-hour charts instead of the hourly to enter.

There is enough commonality between the two systems to make it very easy and natural to add on one after having mastered the other.

There is no point trying to master your psychology until you have settled on a proven trading system that suits your lifestyle and personality. When you have found it, then the work begins!

Create the Correct Trading Environment

Firstly, I want to explain what I mean by the correct trading environment. It does not just refer to your physical trading space although it certainly includes it.
It relates to everything physical including your actions taken while trading your system. Let me give you an example so you can see what I mean.
Let me relate this to the Trade around Your Job system which uses four hour and daily charts. I am lucky enough to have a separate office where my trading platform is situated but you don't need it!

Trading Structure for the Trade Around Your Job System

I go into my office and open my charts at 10 pm on Sunday, Monday, Tuesday, Wednesday, and Thursday night to look for a daily setup.
I use a specific set of rules to find the correct daily set up. Those rules are in a printed sheet on my wall and on a document on the desktop of my computer.
When I find a daily setup, I switch to four-hour checking, I check the charts at 8am, 12pm, 4pm, 8pm and 12 am GMT.
If an entry appears, I look at the printed conditions for entry, on my wall or on the desktop to check. If it is a valid entry, I take my calculator and work out how much of my account to risk on this trade.
I then open my trading platform which is different from my charting platform and enter the trade, putting in my stop loss, I also put in a take profit of 7-10 times my risk in case something happens which drives price an unusual amount.

I then set a trading text message alert for 5 times my risk, I then close the platform, close the trading computer and do something else. (I force myself to do this even though I really want to stay and stare at the charts. I know if I do that, I am likely to get anxious and exit the trade by talking myself out of it.)
If the text alert goes off, I reopen the platform and start trailing my stop loss depending on the different factors which I outline in my Trade around Your Job book.

At 10pm I open the charts again to check for a daily setup and check the progress of my trade. If the correct price action has taken place, I will move my stop loss to break even.
The following day I will check the charts at 10pm where I also look for more daily setups and if applicable, I trail the stop loss I will repeat this checking until I am stopped out. I then bring up my trading records and create a physical record of the trade in my trading record book and an excel spread sheet.

I have created a physical structure comprising a set of behaviors in a physical place (my office) based around The Trade Around Your Job System.
The Trade Around Your Job system trades take place around 2-6 times per month. I have structured my set of behaviors to spend as little time as possible at the computer screen. These behaviors form a physical structure that I focus on.

If I find a flaw in this structure, or if I am not able to adhere to this structure, then I work on tweaking the structure or my behaviors so I can act in as robotic and structured a manner as possible. This structure provides the physical success environment for my trading. My focus and aim is to create an environment and set of behaviors that allow me to stick as closely as possible to my trading plan. I also have other structures related to other parts of my trading. So, what does this mean to you? Well in step 1 you made sure you had a trading system that fitted your trading style.

In step 2 you create a physical environment that allows you to trade this system as perfectly as is humanly possible. One of the purposes of your trading records is to find the stumbling blocks in your behavior and in your system that prevent you from doing this.

Remove Your Focus

It is also wise to have other absorbing activities that take you away from the charts, so your mind is automatically switched to something else. I know of two husband and wife traders who work in IT and both work at their computers full time. When a trade setup comes via software that they created, they take the trade and just continue with their job. What is fantastic about this is that the professional detachment is built in both by removing their focus and by not having to financially depend on trading.

I know another day-trader who plays computer games while waiting for a setup, all the excitement and adrenaline that losing day traders search for, is provided by the game so the actual taking of the trade can be done as professionally as possible.

Overcoming your Faulty Trading Behaviours

You should find at this stage that you are already beginning to think about trading in a more professional fashion. You should have a more realistic view of what trading can and can't give you and you should have set your trading goal.

Your first trading goal should be to create a consistent set of behaviors and to tweak your system until it is profitable.

Notice that this goal is a process goal and not a results goal; you have full control over process goals.

You need to completely forgo results thinking and instead adopt process thinking. If you focus on being the very best trader you can be and have faith that if you do this you will become profitable, then you are thinking right.

Remember, this process involves Kaizen, continuous small improvements compounded to make huge positive changes. Even if when you start, your system is at break-even or even losing a little bit; by using these methods you know that you can turn the system into a winning formula.

It is vital that you keep records about everything you can when taking a trade because the better the information you have the more targeted the changes you can make.

It is also very important to start being aware of your thoughts when you are around your trading platform. If you are at the beginning of this process, either because you are a beginning trader or a trader that has had to take a break because you have gone so far off track, then my suggestion is that you go back to demo trading or use a micro – account. This will save you money and make sure that you are profitable before you add money to your account. If after reading this you feel inner resistance because you want to make money fast, then you are not thinking like a pro trader.

You want to root out those thoughts and bring them to light. They will tell you what stage you are at in the journey from amateur to pro.

The 'trading pro' is self –aware and you need to be aware of your thoughts in order to change them.
You need to be able to mentally stand aside from yourself in order to observe your thoughts rather than just think them. How do you take control of your mind in this way? daily meditation!
There are different types of meditation; however, the one you want to do is the simple clearing of your mind type. Simply sit comfortably for a period of time, say you start with 5 minutes, and then build it up to about 30 minutes a day. Clear your mind of all thoughts and imagine an image such as a clear blue sky. When thoughts pop into your mind, clear them away so your mind is empty. This will be hard to do at first but becomes easier with practice.
This trains your mind to 'see' thoughts rather than just to think them. There are many other benefits to meditation, just find yourself a good basic book or look on YouTube for some guidance if you want more information.

The 80/20 Principle

If you have never read the 80-20 Principle by Richard Koch then I highly recommend you do, it's a great little book. Basically, it describes the phenomenon where all things are not equal. In life about 20% of causes are responsible for 80% of results.

What this means to you as a trader is that there are likely a very few things in your trading that are causing most of the problems. By dealing with those few things, you will gain a disproportionately better result. So how do you find your biggest trading issue?

Well, you probably already know what it is; it is that thing or things that cause you the most frustration. You can probably remember an incident very vividly and painfully caused by this issue. This is where to start. I don't know you personally so I will be covering the different trading behaviors in no particular order.
Just skip ahead so you find the ones that are your biggest problem and start there.
(If for any reason you can't find your particular issue then email me at lrthomasauthor@gmail.com and I'll try to add it to the book)

Negative Trading Behaviours

I have grouped typical negative trading behaviors together, that tend to spring from the same cause.

Not Committed to Your System

When a trader is not really committed to their system these are the typical behaviors listed below.

Searching for the Holy Grail trading system that never loses
Buying trading course after trading course
Being too influenced by other traders

This behavior stems from not having a clear set of criteria when choosing a trading system. The trader just wants to make money and is looking for the magic system that is the RIGHT system for them, ideally a system that never loses and will make them a multi-millionaire in a very short space of time.
Part of the reason for skipping from system to system is a 'grass is always greener 'type of mentality, a fear of missing out by committing to one trading method.
The problem is that years can go by, and you will never run out of systems to try. It is time to stop wasting time and find the method that suits you.
If you carry on you can waste years and never get anywhere. It is time to 'turn pro' and commit!
I have already talked about this in Step 1 of this process, however, now is the time to repeat the reasons for choosing and sticking to a particular trading system.
It is most important to find a system that is right for your personality and lifestyle. This could be an end-of-day trading system, a swing trading style, day trading or even scalping. It is the system that when you have tried it felt the most comfortable for you and gave you the greatest success.
If you own a lot of courses already, then it is very likely that you have that system already sitting on your hard drive. There is no point moving on with any of the exercises in this book until you have found the method that works best for you and that you will commit to. When that happens, don't buy any more courses, don't listen to any more traders, stop visiting forums and clear your mind for this trading process.

Trading Too Many of Everything

Behaviors include...

Trading too many strategies
Trading too many time-frames
Trading too many instruments

The other reason for sticking to one system, which beginner traders completely underestimate, is the amount of complexity inherent in even the simplest system. Entry patterns for example are always slightly different from each other, even if it looks the same, there may be different circumstances that led to this type of entry. Why is this important? Well, you may find in your records that taking a particular entry in one set of conditions gives you a better result, in which case you may risk less on the entry taken in the other type of condition.

It is these levels of complexity within a system that make the difference as to the level of profitability of the system. It is impossible to master these levels of complexity if you are trading too many systems, time frames and instruments. You need to focus on one trading system, and if necessary one instrument and time frame so you can master the different levels of complexity inherent in that system.

When a trader tries to do too much, he will experience trading as a sense of overwhelm. They are doing too much and can't focus because their brain is not able to deal with the amount of information. So why do traders do this?

It is a belief about trading that is a sense of lack; they believe that more is better. If one system can make you money, then three systems can make you more.

If one timeframe makes money then combining swing trading with scalping will make much more money.

If you can make money trading the forex major pairs, then surely you can make more by trading the crosses, the exotics, indices, stocks and commodities.

You see where I'm going with this....

You should only trade as much as you can EASILY handle.

There is a trader I know who makes huge money and only swing trades the EUR/USD. Many pro traders do this. They stick to one pair, one method, and one time frame. The other reason for this is because their brain is not overwhelmed with information, they can really focus on their chosen currency pair and become expert on all its moves.

Not all strategies work with all pairs; even if you just trade one strategy with multiple pairs, (which is easily done with an end of day strategy) you will find that the strategy works better with a few pairs. During the process of Kaizen, you will then automatically restrict yourself to those few pairs in order to increase your win/loss ratio.

Entering Trades Too Early

Entering a trade too early is related to two things, one is a sense of lack about the markets. The thinking goes something like this. 'If I don't get in now price will run away and I will miss this trade. There are only a few trades. What the hell just get in!'

The problem with type of thought process is that it is experienced as a sense of extreme urgency and the trader fails to recognize his thought process because it is happening so fast. The trader then enters the market and often loses because the market is not ready to move yet. The problem then compounds itself because after a couple of these types of entries, the trader may become so disillusioned about the trade that they fail to enter when the decisive move begins.

This leads to the type of thinking that goes something like this. 'I'll never succeed in trading look at that trade I missed, I'm useless at it' this leads to a sense of failure which can then lead to depression.

This type of behavior can repeat itself over and over unless the trader changes the way they deal with the problem.

The Physical Method

The way to deal with this problem is two-fold, firstly you deal with the physical behaviors and at the same time you deal with the emotional feelings.
Dealing with the physical side of things means that in a very conscious manner you put physical obstacles in your way so that it becomes a lot more difficult to self-sabotage.
If you normally rush to the charts when an alert goes off, or if you are watching the charts when a trade entry sets up, then you deliberately step away from the charts.

Now this is going to feel uncomfortable, because everything inside you will be screaming to take the entry. However, this is the time when you want to slow things down. Have your written entry conditions on a piece of card and take that card and read it over carefully, away from the charts. This will confirm that you are right for taking that extra time and make sure you are not missing anything.
While you are doing this take deep breaths and do the emotional exercises listed below to calm yourself.
When you feel calm, and you are sure in your mind what you are looking for as an entry point you can return to check the screen.

Now if you are trading with the longer time frames, it might take hours or even days for the correct entry to show itself. Note the type of behaviors you show in this scenario.
It may be that you have a price alert that goes off long before your actual confirmed entry.

However, your behavior is such that you start staring at the screen and the infinitesimal moves of the market and then you talk yourself into entering before the actual confirmation.
In this type of scenario, you need to force yourself to check the screen rather than watch the screen. This type of forced checking can also be used with the lower time frames.
Let's say you need to enter on the close of the 4-hour candle, the price alert has gone off, but instead of checking the screen you check your watch. You then see that there is 2 hours to go before the close of the next four-hour candle. (If this is a short-term trade, this could be a 15-minute candle)

You find something to do away from the screen, making sure that however much that sense of urgency impels you to open the charts you are deliberately ignoring it and taking control of your actions, at the same time you do the emotional exercises.
Set a time alarm if necessary and return to the screen at the close of the candle. When you look at the charts have your entry criteria to hand so you can physically check if your entry criteria are met.
This helps with the urge to enter as if you can physically see that your criteria are not met by written evidence it will be harder for your mind to rationalize.

Be mentally prepared for checking rather than watching. Checking means a quick look and check to see if your entry criteria are met, if not met, close the charts, and set your alerts until the close of the next candle.
You need to avoid watching the charts at these times because the urgency to enter the market can become overwhelming and will lead to loss of control.
By deliberately structuring your physical actions so that you spend as little time as possible in front of the charts you are building a set of habits that will protect you from self-sabotage. These habits will feel strange at first but after a few times of implementing this new process it will just become a part of your trading routine.

The Emotional Method

The tool I use for this is known as EFT short for emotional freedom technique. This technique was developed by a man called Gary Craig some years back and is the most powerful method I know for reducing the impact of powerful emotions sometimes in a matter of a few minutes. The other virtue of this method is that it extremely simple to do and can be done by anyone.

To give you an idea of the power of this method I am including a link to a video of some EFT therapists using EFT with soldiers with Post Traumatic Stress Disorder. These soldiers had suffered with this disorder since the Vietnam war and more than 20 years later traditional psychotherapy had done very little to help.

I suggest you take a few minutes to watch the video to see what I mean, before continuing with the book.

You can find all links on the resource page of my blog.

https://traderselfcontrol.com/resources/

You can see from the video that even psychiatrists and psychologists admit the power of using EFT to reduce harmful emotions.

By combining the power of EFT with behavioral modification in your trading you will see considerable improvements in both your behavior and the emotional pulls that cause it.

How to Do EFT

EFT is easy to do; you simply tap yourself lightly with your first two fingers on some specific acupuncture points. While you are tapping you are focusing on the thing that is giving you pain and repeating it out loud. The way you measure improvement is to give the emotion a number between 1-10 and measure after each round of tapping how far the emotions have reduced.

The specific acupuncture points are…
The karate chop, at the side of the hand
The inside tip of the eyebrow
The side of the eye
Under the eye
Under the nose
Under the mouth
The collar bone
Under the arm pit (you zero in on the slightly painful area)

I am including a link to a YouTube video that shows you the basics visually which makes it much easier to see exactly where these places are and how to tap.
https://traderselfcontrol.com/resources/

When you tap for your trading issues you need to find a phrase that most closely describes these issues for you. You can replace the words I use with those of your own that more closely describe your feelings.

Now let's get back to the first problem, entering a trade too early and dealing with the sense of urgency that makes us want to enter the trade too early.

Here is the EFT tapping protocol remember you can substitute words that more closely describe the emotions you feel. This protocol should be done when you are feeling the emotion of urgency to enter a trade.

The best way to summon up the emotions is to actually be in the situation while you are doing it.

The other way is to run a mental movie in your mind that reproduces a specific event where you felt this high level of urgency. As you run the movie, when you get to the part where you feel this high sense of urgency try and build it up to as high a level as possible to represent most closely what you felt during an actual trade. When you feel this heightened emotion give it a number and then do this round of tapping.

EFT Round One

While tapping the karate point repeat 3 times.

Even though I feel such a strong sense of urgency to enter a trade too early I deeply and completely love and accept myself.

Even though I feel such a strong sense of urgency to enter a trade too early I deeply and completely love and accept myself.

Even though I feel such a strong sense of urgency to enter a trade too early I deeply and completely love and accept myself.

Lightly tapping the eyebrow point about 7 times while saying…

I need to enter the trade right now even though it's not the right time.

Tap the side of the eye about 7 times while saying…

I mustn't miss this trade; it may get away and I will lose out.

Tap underneath the eye about 7 times…

I have to enter the trade right now to make myself feel better.

Tap under the nose about 7 times...
I feel such a strong feeling that it is really vital that I enter the trade right now.
Tap under the mouth above the chin about 7 times...
I know I shouldn't enter this trade too early but I feel that I need to.
Tap just under the collar bone about 7 times ...
I have to enter the trade to make myself feel better and I don't want to lose out, maybe I'll never get this chance again.
Tap under the arm pit where it feels a bit sore about 7 times...
I want to enter the trade, I may lose this chance forever and never make a living trading.

(Notice that in the EFT round I also added the thoughts that I had around this issue.)
When you have finished the first round of tapping take your emotional temperature and see if you are still at a high figure when you replay that event in your mind. Repeat the tapping round until you feel that your emotional temperature has reduced to about 1 or zero. You should feel there is no sense of urgency to enter the charts and that in fact you have plenty of time.
You should also have had a paradigm shift so that you simply think differently about the issue. You may now find that you think that there is no point entering a trade unless you can do a low-risk entry and if the price moves too fast and you miss the entry then you will look for an opportunity later in the move to enter.
When you have this type of paradigm shift, and you feel no sense of urgency to enter the charts too early then test it out on a real trade.
You may find that the sense of urgency re-emerges because of the different situation. Simply do your rounds of tapping in the same way using phrases that most exactly describe what you are feeling. You should combine this tapping with the physical actions you are taking to remove yourself from the charts into another place.

The other thing that may happen while you are tapping is that while this issue fades, other issues start to emerge. You may have a memory or a thought that relates to a feeling of lack or missing out. Maybe you lived in a household where your parents were always worried about money, and you have a specific memory related to a parent.
Firstly before tapping on this next issue make sure you have completely cleared the issue you are working on.
Then you can do another round of tapping related to the sense of lack in your life and the specific family memory that popped up.

Example

Even though my dad said 'we are poor, and we'll always be poor' I completely love and accept myself.

The important thing to remember is that even if you feel you are not doing it 'right' EFT is very forgiving, and you will get results.

So, to recap, we find the issues that are having the most negative impact on our trading. We design a set of physical behaviors that will make it difficult to self-sabotage. We integrate those behaviors into a trading routine. We perform this trading routine even though it may feel a bit strange. We use strategies like checking and timing the candles instead of watching the charts. We can also use text price alerts where we set price alerts at just past the breakout area so we don't even touch the charts until after a breakout. You can design your own set of trading behaviors that do the job, anything that makes it physically difficult to self-sabotage is fine.

We also use EFT to deal with the emotional issues and neutralize them, so we have a different paradigm and no longer wish to repeat this negative behavior.

Entering Trades Too Late

Here we have the issue of watching trades run away from us. This is the downside of too much analysis and a tremendous fear of being wrong about the trade. Over-analysis is when the trading conditions are all met, the setup and the entry conditions are met and yet the traders mind is still looking for further proof that he is right. They have not really accepted the unknown nature of the 'hard right edge of the charts.'
When there is too much fear attached to the outcome of the trade it usually comes after a series of losses. Now if the trader has been sticking to their proven method, then the consequences of this type of losing streak are that it could end at any time. A logical way of dealing with this issue is to measure the longest recorded series of losses for that system and when a loss takes place mentally accept that it may be the beginning of a string of losses equivalent to the longest recorded losing streak.

There is a trader I know who takes a break from trading if they have three losses in a row. They know if that happens something is off with their trading and this removal from the trading arena has saved their account.
However, there are also losses which are the normal part of a trading system, and the trader needs to be able to deal with them.
One of the issues of too much analysis is attaching the outcome of any particular trade to the imagined long-term outcome of failing in the markets. For example, the traders mind could be telling them,
'If I lose this trade, it shows I shouldn't be trading the markets, I am no good at trading, and how am I going to tell my wife? I haven't earned money this month, I'll have to give up trading and get a job, how can I get a job at my age? We'll lose the house and be out on the street and then my wife will leave me; I will end up a bum living on the streets.'

Is it any wonder that with this type of thought process a trader can be frozen with fear?

Thus, a reluctance to enter the markets leads to late entries into trades, which leads to losses. It also leads to talking oneself out of trades which should be taken, leading to missed winners. This leads to skewing the normal statistics of the trading system which can turn a winning system into a losing system. This then leads to extreme fear when entering the markets which can lead to a frozen trigger finger where a trader is emotionally and physically unable to enter a trade.

How to Deal with Over-Analysis, the Physical Method

This involves the trader creating a sequence of events and sticking to the sequence without much thought. To reduce the anxiety, it helps to reduce the position size of the trade.
On a piece of card write a list of the steps of the trade with little tick boxes next to each step. The goal of the trader is to complete the steps on the card. This way trader only has to focus on each little step at a time and manage the fear of each little part which makes it much less overwhelming.

This changes the goals from results goals like winning the next trade which is out of the trader's control to completing each trading step and ticking each box which are process goals. This can give the trader a much-needed sense of achievement and get them back on track.

By trading as they should be trading, they are more likely to win trades, by winning trades they feel a sense of achievement which encourages them to continue with the correct trading behaviors.

In this physical method the adherence to the tick boxes is designed to override the traders' feelings of fear and tendency to over analyze the trades.

However, the use of the emotional method is what causes the trader to have a paradigm shift which makes the steps much easier. We will cover that next.

The Emotional Method

When using the EFT rounds below, create a mental movie of a specific incident in your mind. This movie should take about 30 seconds to one minute going through the whole of the trading sequence.

The emotional crescendo of this mental movie is where you find yourself unable to enter the trade and watching the trade run away from you. Measure the emotions from 1-10, you want them as high as possible and then check on the level with each round of tapping.

You will know you have succeeded when the level is down to 0 or 1 when you are replaying the mental movie in your head. You should also have a paradigm shift where your thoughts about the issue change. You may think something along the lines of

'I don't know what the results of the trade will be, that's not my job. I know the system works over time, my job is just to take each trade to the best of my ability'. This will show that you have had a complete change of beliefs around the issue.

You may find that the fears resurface when it is time to enter a real trade, just tap as you did during the practice session. Even if you miss this trade while tapping, by the next trade you should find the issue is resolved.

You may also find that while tapping for this issue, other memories and thoughts arise that are connected to the issue that need dealing with. Make sure you have resolved this particular issue before you go on to the next. The type of thing that could come up would be a foundational one such as memories of a parent saying something like.

'that's too risky we don't take risks with our money' or memories such as parents talking about financial issues with a lot of fear.'

The Emotional Method for Analysis-Paralysis and the Fear of Being Wrong

Remember you can input your own phrase that most closely describes the issue

While tapping the karate point repeat 3 times.

Even though I feel so much fear before I enter a trade I deeply and completely love and accept myself.

Even though I feel so much fear before I enter a trade I deeply and completely love and accept myself.

Even though I feel so much fear before I enter a trade I deeply and completely love and accept myself.

Lightly tapping the eyebrow point about 7 times while saying...

I'm too scared to enter the trade I need to know what is going to happen.

Tap the side of the eye about 7 times while saying...

I need more time to think about this trade, I wish I knew what would happen.

Tap underneath the eye about 7 times...

I want to see into the future with this trade will it be a winner.

Tap under the nose about 7 times...

If this trade loses then it means I am a rubbish trader and I can't provide for my family.

Tap under the mouth above the chin about 7 times...

This trade must be a winner, but I am so scared in case it loses.

Tap just under the collar bone about 7 times...

I can't risk losing this trade, if it loses it means I am a loser who can't provide.

Tap under the arm pit where it feels a bit sore about 7 times...

I want to wait before I enter the trade until I know for sure it will win.

As you can see in the above EFT round, I put in the thoughts around the issue of not entering the trade.
By articulating the thoughts out loud it also helps the trader to logically as well as emotionally process their irrationality. It is also very common for other issues to come up such as fear of not being able to provide.

If these thoughts flash into your mind while tapping, then clear the issue you are working on and then work on the 'fear of not being able to provide 'or other issues.

Frozen Trigger Finger 'Can't Take the Trade'

Sometimes the fear of entering the trade has grown so strong that it has become a full-fledged phobia and the trader is literally unable to enter the trade.
With this situation the physical method does not work, what is needed is emotional work to destroy the phobia.
I would advise calling in a professional who specializes in phobia cures and ideally understands the trading environment. However, if you are stuck and you want to have a go yourself then try these methods below.

The NLP Phobia Cure

Find a quiet place to be by yourself while you do this exercise.
Imagine you are sitting by yourself in a movie theatre with a huge movie screen in front of you and the projector behind and above you where a projectionist would normally sit.
Then in your mind's eye see yourself float out of your seat and into the projectionist's booth where you can see yourself sitting in the movie theatre.
You then watch yourself watching a movie describing the sequence of events which led up to you being unable to pull the trigger on the trade.
Watch the movie through in your mind's eye; this should take no longer than 30 seconds to a minute.
Then rewind the film very fast back to the beginning and play it again. Do this three times.

Then play the movie again but instead of the movie being silent this time add in your imagination some very fast and cheerful music like circus music or anything you like.
Then play the movie again but this time if the movie was in color change it to black and white, turn it upside down and play it still with the happy music.

All this time this should be done while you are watching yourself watching the screen.
This exercise is designed to scramble this series of events in your mind, so it doesn't have the same emotional impact. Wait for a few minutes after doing this exercise and then run through the movie where you froze when it came to taking the entry again and see if the intensity of the emotion has lifted.

The EFT Phobia Cure

Before doing this exercise measure the level of intensity you feel when visualizing yourself entering a trade. Run the mental movie again in your head. When you reach the emotional crescendo part of the movie where you are about to enter a trade, keep doing tapping rounds until the intensity has reduced. Repeat until all intensity has gone and you have had a paradigm shift where you think differently about entering a trade. For example, you may find yourself thinking, 'entering a trade is just the risk you have to take in trading, you just do the best you can'.

Then test it on a real trade, keep tapping while you are waiting for the entry until you have reduced the fear around entering the trade.

At this point let me relate a warning story of what happened to me when I did this exercise, I completely removed my fear of entering a trade, to the point where I had the opposite problem of entering trades too boldly. If this issue arises after you have cured your fear then you must tap on the issue of entering trades incautiously. You need caution followed by boldness only when you know the trade is right!

I must emphasize that my advice is to see a professional EFT therapist, after all it is your career at stake, and you would likely only need one or two sessions to resolve the issue.

Compounding Negative Behaviours in Complete Loss of Control

The next set of behaviors can be grouped together as they represent the same basic cause, a complete loss of control. The problem is one of compounding where if you lose control at the beginning of the trade, that loss of control tends to compound and other behaviours come into play.

Trading outside the strategy.
Forcing trades, talking yourself into taking a trade that doesn't exist.
Trading without a stop loss.
Moving the stop loss further away.
Risking too much on a trade.
Revenge trading trying to get back at the markets.
Closing the trade too early, not allowing it to play itself out.

For example, you are impatient for a trade, so you force a trade, entering in the markets when there is no real trade to take. When the trade moves against you, you move your stop loss further away. The loss compounds and when you finally exit the market you have lost a good portion of your account. In a rage at the markets, you have a 'don't care attitude' and start risking too much on trades that don't exist and taking imaginary revenge against the market. You start trading without stops and next thing you know you are margined out, all because you lost control and got impatient for a trade.

The problem here is that human beings are not wired to maintain self-control for long periods of time.

If you are day trading and staring at the charts for over 2 hours you are quite likely to start losing your self-control. Some traders lose self-control trading hourly charts, some even higher time frames.

If you are wired to be a short-term day trader but you start giving back money to the market after 2 hours, then only trade for an hour and a half.

Don't trade until you get exhausted, stop while you still have a reasonable degree of mental energy.

One of the biggest ways to increase your level of self-control is to increase the time frames you trade.

If you switch to trading end-of-day charts, then you are unlikely to lose control because too much time is involved.

You check your charts at the end of the trading day, you have ample time to do your research, and there is generally no need to worry about news announcements. When you enter a trade, you know that you can't see any results until the following day, so it is much easier to close the trading platform and go to bed.

The point I am making is that if you find yourself regularly losing control in the markets then you very likely need to switch to a higher time frame.

If you feel resistance to this change then there is a belief about making money in the markets that is causing a conflict. It is common for traders to believe that the more they trade the more money they will make. They also believe that the harder they work the more they earn. These beliefs are related to how most people earn money, via a job and can lead to over trading and reluctance to move up in time frames where there are less trading opportunities. Logically they may know they will make more money trading higher time frames but emotionally they feel drawn to scalping and day trading even though those time frames cause them to lose control and their money.

Before we go on to the tapping round for dealing with these beliefs let's take a logical look at the belief that you can make more money by day trading or scalping than by trading the longer time frames.

Firstly, let me ask why you got into trading in the first place, was it just to make money or was it to increase your quality of life. When you see rows of bank traders chained to their desks, does that look like quality of life? Those traders burn out very fast because of the high stress environment.

In order to make money in the markets you need to be profitable, if you keep losing control in the markets you can't be profitable. It doesn't matter that you may know a scalper or day trader making thousands a day. If that is not how you are wired to trade the markets, then what makes them money could lose all your money. You are better off to give them your money to trade while you go off and do something else.

When you find a method that gives you the lifestyle you want and is a fit for your personality, then you are much more likely to make money. That method includes the time frame that allows you to trade without loss of control.

The Emotional Method

The emotional method for dispelling beliefs that more trading equals more profit in the markets.

Remember you can input your own phrase that most closely describes the issue.

While tapping the karate point repeat 3 times.

Even though I believe that I need to take lots of trades to make money in the markets I deeply and completely love and accept myself.

Even though I believe that I need to take lots of trades to make money in the markets I deeply and completely love and accept myself.

Even though I believe that I need to take lots of trades to make money in the markets I deeply and completely love and accept myself.

Lightly tapping the eyebrow point about 7 times while saying…

I believe that the harder I work the more money I'll make even though I really know that isn't true.

Tap the side of the eye about 7 times while saying…

If I work hard the market will reward me, the harder I work the more reward I get.

Tap underneath the eye about 7 times…

By staying in the market even though I am mentally tired I believe the market will reward me. Hard work always reaps a reward.

Tap under the nose about 7 times…

If I trade 8 hours a day then I can make big money in trading.

Tap under the mouth above the chin about 7 times…

The harder I work the more money I will make.

Tap just under the collar bone about 7 times…

Taking more trades means I am working hard and hard workers will be rewarded.

Tap under the arm pit where it feels a bit sore about 7 times…

The more I trade the more I will earn.

When you have finished the first round of tapping say out loud to yourself, the harder I work the more money I make and see how true it sounds on a scale of 1-10. You should repeat the tapping rounds until that statement doesn't feel true for you anymore.

Wrap Up

Now you know the method for taking back your self- control in the markets.
Where possible create a physical system that makes it difficult to self-sabotage.
Combine this with EFT to reduce emotional intensity, change your beliefs and create a paradigm shift that benefits your trading.

If you want to go deeper into how to improve your trading mindset you can find my full training at https://traderselfcontrol.com

All resources for this book are found at https://traderselfcontrol.com/resources
.
If there is anything else, you would like to see in this book that I haven't covered contact me via my email address lrthomasauthor@gmail.com

Conclusion

I really appreciate reviews, so if you found this book worthwhile, please leave a review telling other readers how this book has helped you.
If you have any questions about the system, then feel free to email me and you will get as swift an answer as I can give.

I wish you good trading.
LR Thomas

Recommended Resources

https://traderselfcontrol.com/resources/

Notes

Notes

Notes

Notes

Notes

Notes

Notes

Notes

Notes

Notes

Notes

Notes

Notes

Notes

Notes

Notes

Notes

Notes

Notes

Notes

Notes

Notes

Notes

Notes

Notes

Notes

Notes

Notes

www.ingramcontent.com/pod-product-compliance
Lightning Source LLC
LaVergne TN
LVHW022320200926
848481LV00004B/1377
9798201746865